MW00426139

Also by Robert L. Giron

Wrestling with Wood

Impressions françaises

Recuerdos

Metamorphosis of the Serpent God

———

Robert L. Giron

[signature]

Gival Press

Published by Gival Press an imprint of Gival Press, LLC. For information please write: Gival Press, LLC, P. O. Box 3812, Arlington, VA 22203.

First Editon ISBN 1-928589-07-3

Acknowledgments

"Fallen Feather" was published in *Poets of '74*, Quest Publications, 1974.

An earlier version of "Living Shadows in the Present" was published in *Carta de Chicano Studies-o-El Chuco News*, University of Texas at El Paso, 1977.

"Ode to the Pacific" was published in *Best Poets of the 20th Century on Man & Environment*, Winston-Paramount Books, 1975.

"Playing Cowboys Mexican Style, 1958" was published in *A Muse to Follow*, The National Library of Poetry, 1966.

"Water for Pancho Villa at El Río Grande" was published in *The Texas Anthology*, San Houston University Press, 1979; previously it was published in *El Conquistador*, El Paso Community College, 1978.

"Rita, the Old Woman" was published in *El Conquistador*, El Paso Community College, 1979.

"Old Woman Gazing" was published in *Chrysalis*, El Paso Community College, 1977.

"Cristo Rey" was published in *Art Form Magazine*, 1977.

"Heartwretched Man" was published in *Slouching Towards Consensus*, 1994; previously it was published in *The Poet's Domain: A Place for the Genuine*, ROAD Publishers, 1990.

"Tex-Mex Poetic Roundup" was published in *Austin Writers*, 1992.

"Kinsmen" was published in *The Best Poems of the '90s*, The National Library of Poetry, 1996.

"Unwrapping like an Egyptian Mummy" was published in *Amphora Review*, 1981.

"Stonehenge in a Not-So-Distant Time" was published in *Slouching Towards Consensus*, 1995.

"Ménage à Trois" was published in *This Week in Texas*, Asylum Enterprises, 1983.

"The Goodbye" was published in *This Week in Texas*, Asylum Enterprises, 1983.

"Ash Wednesday" was published in *Poets of '76*, Quest Publications, 1977.

"One Afternoon in the Cathedral" was published in *El Conquistador*, El Paso Community College, 1978.

"The Olive Branch" was published in *Art Form Magazine*, 1977.

"City of Angles and Cubes" was published in *Goodbye Dove*, The University of Texas at El Paso, 1972.

"Memories" was published in *A Gathering of Friends*, Montgomery College, 1993.

"Lovesong of a Spoken Love", "The Response to a Spoken Love", "Twilight", and "Yesterday I Saw a Naked Body" were published in *The Great Lawn*, Spring 1997.

For Ken, amigo del alma

Contents

Part 1
–
Quetzalcoatl
the Serpent God

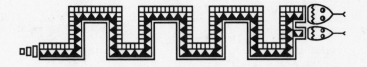

Quetzacoatl the Serpent God

Quetzacoatl the Serpent God of the Aztecs,
with royal plumage to match his stature
led his people. The Aztecs believed he
would come again to join his people, echoes
of the messiah, yet when Cortés and his fleet
appeared Cortés was taken to be Quetzacoatl
and so the natives prostrated themselves in
awe of their god. La Malinche, courtesan to
Cortés, was thought to be the traitor of her
people but Xicanas of Aztlán declare her a
savior of her people. How will history set
the record? Pestilence, small pox, and
Spanish gun powder were stronger than the
blood of virgins to defeat the European
Crown. Yet if Native and Spanish had not
joined in peace or love would Mexico be
what it is today? Are the mother country's
thighs that chose to survive worthy of
contempt when if they had not opened up to
the throbbing future they perhaps would
have languished and died in the past?
The desire to continue and live is far
greater than to capitulate without hope,
to resurrect the phoenix, and to shed a
new skin again albeit changed from its

original hide. Today Quetzacoatl crawls
along the earth from Tenochtitlán to the
northern land, and along the way he leaves
his scales *de colores* among his people and
the matriarchs of the vibrant *raza* collect
them to quilt the fabric that envelops
European and Native and all the other
blood from veins that make up the
sacred people of Quetzacoatl and his
union to survive all, even death.

Tiquan Ovens

Give us this day our daily bread
and forgive us our trespasses as we
forgive those who trespass on our land.

Along the Cliff Dwellings

Within the realm of brittle woods and icy-cold
streams caressed by serene north wind around
the ancient fire lies the modern primitive clique.

As the shadows lengthen and the fragile pine cones
flare by spontaneous combustion casting a skeleton
against ashes, frightened deer chase the grizzly
bear back into the abandoned caves.

Crackling and fizzling, the warmth of the
ever-changing fire keeps pace with rushing
water of the dam erected where once lived the tribe.

The First Thanksgiving

On the banks of the Río Grande now
    San Elizario, El Paso, Texas,
then the land of the natives, the Spanish
    praised God for their
source of water and safe journey through
    the hot treacherous
Chihuahuan desert of New Spain.

After nearly four months of torturous pain,
    the procession of
eighty three ox-drawn, wooden-wheeled
    wagons and carts reached
the river on 20 April 1598. Determined
    to stay, the colonizers
traveled with seven thousand head of cattle,
    sheep, goats, oxen,
and horses. Though weary and exhausted,
    they rested, waiting
for the jubilant celebration.

Then, on 30 April 1598 after the mass for
    the Feast of the
Ascension, Don Juan de Oñate took
    possession of the land and all

that it contained for the Crown of Spain
    and ultimately for fame.

Replete with food and drink, the more than
    five hundred and thirty
brave souls commemorated the day, for
    Marcos Farfán de los Godos'
drama was staged to praise the friars who
    converted the natives
for the Church of New Spain.

All this was documented to gain the land
    for Spain twenty-two years
before the Pilgrims landed at Plymouth,
    and so in 1598 on the banks
of the Río Grande the First Thanksgiving
    took place in Texas.

Fallen Feather

I went by the park
and saw my friend Littlefoot;
she said not a word.
I began to speak,
but she laid her finger
upon my lips and handed
me her burial feather.

Living Shadows in the Present

The Olmecs, the Toltecs, and the Zapotecs
—gone, but not really.
Moctezuma king and god of Tenochtitlán—
Huitzilopochtli war god sacred to the
     Aztecs—
All of this changed by Cortés
thought to be Quetzalcoatl.
And this in turn readjusted by Juárez
who gave birth to the Mestizo
who is now a Chicano
who speaks only English.

Ode to the Pacific

Softly you spoke out
and the tide heeled
coming slowly upon
the beach,
creeping and softly
approaching.
Now, as the ships
sail upon your waves
you speak harshly,
and roar your name
briskly coming to shore
deceivingly taking
men from under their feet
into your inner womb.

Eruption

Twisted inside out,
trapped deep within the
earth, we
erupt in contempt.

Dry Cotton

Swallow fiber
dry as a day in August,
then hope for rainwater.

TriPoem

1.

The destiny of time lies
with tribes as they shatter
the remaining reflections of
opium dreams and wade through
the mist of dissonant harmonies.

2.

A moment comes and passes
while the want to touch and sense
the past is only
a spoken myth among the
unknown chronicles of lost gods.

3.

Tenets have become lyrated
and geniuses of immortality
pizzicate the strings of infamy.

Oracle

prophets taste the earth
nations spit them out
    afire—
no law is grounded

Part 2

–

Walking on Cactus

Mi Tierra

The weathervane pointed west and
thousands passed by in their wagons.
But here I will stay where the
vineyards have turned to cactus
and the cross marks my bond
    to *mi tierra*.

Cosmos in the El Paso Desert

One comes from the same source,
yet like the leaves on the tree
we are different, and upon the
    earth
we search for our land; life
is like the dew that falls on a crisp
day, yet while in the desert only
the silk of the cobweb can lead us
back to the labyrinth of our stay.

Heartbeat

for Tía

With cane in hand
she walked the path
of the single golden ray.

Alone but attentive
to the chirping of the birds,
she would knit the day away.

With Elizabeth Taylor perfection,
she would prepare herself for her
public yet no one could capture
the mystery of her fiery eyes.

Patience formed her world
and the laughter of children
fed her maternal instinct.

Grandma

Keeping in step with
time, she endured.
A boulder beneath
angels' falls.

Gray crossed brown,
branches of twilight
nesting on her head.

Tranquil she seemed,
yet storms of anguish
lodged in her side.

Sentry of her garden,
she pulled weeds
choking flowers
of her content.

Ánimo

—Do your work with *ánimo*.

Yes, Grandpa. I coughed
in the smoke-filled room
with yellow-glossed
picture frames.
Gasping for air, I
rubbed raw eye tissue
wanting to break the dam.

—In the '30s
there wasn't much to do.
I would hop on train cars
and travel to my content,
would stop and work,
lay some oil pipe,
play a little poker,
free drinks all around—
I was popular then and even now,
though it's not like it used to be.
Can't even play penny ante,
it's just for fun,
but before two or five hundred dollars
seemed like small time.

Then a tear, two, three.

    —Better tell your grandma
      to check those eyes.

Another cup of coffee,
another Prince Edward rolled to perfection,
another coat of yellow gloss
on picture frames
resting in silence.

Playing Cowboys Mexican Style, 1958

The cool October wind chilled our fingers as
we held onto the reins, yet we continued our El Paso
play, branding the dry clay with our signatures.
I was the townspeople with land and cattle;
we would fight to the end in our OK corral.
Villa drafted the poor, promised them the world,
killed those he couldn't persuade. With the house
broom as my horse and my aunt's cane as my rifle,
we fought until Villa and I stood facing each other,
waiting for John Wayne to settle the dispute. But
usually a call for hot cocoa ended the feud.

Water for Pancho Villa at El Río Grande

1.

We heard the pounding of hoofs racing
    towards El Río Grande;
far off a gust of wind encircled the
    mesquites.

2.

Mother said to stand quiet and draw the
    water.

3.

I held my breath; mother crossed herself. I
almost fell in, much rain this season. Never
    looking up
I tightened the eartheen jars to the support
    and prayed.

4.

Mother stood between me and the
    horsemen and asked:
"A drink to quench your thirst?"

Villa answered, "From the cup of the little
    one.
To quench my thirst."
Hands shaking, I made my offering.
"*Gracias*. Such a lovely creature, your
    daughter, *señora*."
Mother nodded, crossed herself as we stood
    embraced by wind.

Rita, the Old Woman

1.

Rita cleaned table tops with
a dirty, wet rag; would ring it
and shake it dry, droppings on the
      floor.

2.

Her husband counted her
      underwear,
never let her wash them out in
      public,
hung them behind the outhouse
protected by mesquites.

3.

Comrades discussed the fall of
      hail,
damage done to cotton fields.

4.

Rita prepared coffee,
guests waited.

5.

Soltero cursed the hail;
women rolled their eyes and men
puffed on their cigars.

6.

All stared at the coffee pot,
boiling water taking a forth
      cooling.

7.

Pulling out his watch, Soltero
      declared:
"When you finish talking, please
      shut off the
light."

8.

Rita paced ready to clean
the table top.

Doña's Cross

Flying into Nebraska, I couldn't
help but think that the land is
barren. Only a Catapillar tractor
east of the Scottsbluff monument
and the Great Western sugar stack
stand like pyramids in the prairie.
Not a single neon light
welcomes the early sunset against
the snow dressed buildings.
On toward Mitchell, we pass
the cemetery and I notice a
white cross resting on its side.
Doña is buried there. The woman
who jay-walked with purse under
arm and who stopped traffic
without a clue. During mass, she prayed
aloud and lighted candles while father
gave the sermon. Some thought her insane.
I grew to like her toothless smile and
admired her strength of character.

Old Woman Gazing

I sat and eyed the campers
while they mustered up their wood.
The children opened wide
swallowing restless wind
ruffling the branches of the pine.
The evening crawled
as it touched the tree tops
and the frigid old woman set
brittle pine and birch afire.
She squatted and gazed
into the crackling flames,
before her was an image
wrinkled and scorched by time;
troubled by a sense of regret,
she drank from the wine bottle
and laughed as she spat into
the flames.

A Remedy

A cold wind grew
while Jr. and I played
cops and robbers—he the robber
    and I,
of course, the cop—
but I was trapped
and thrown against the shed
to find a splinter in my palm.
Running, I yelled:
"Tía, help me" and
you, the good aunt,
would say:
    "Cure yourself little
    frog tail by farting
    today and tomorrow"
and with uncontrollable laughter
I would forget the pain
and run back to the shed
for instant replay.

Bluebird

Everything is packed
and ready to go.
I hear popcorn popping in the background.
Yes, I know the house is for sale.
I recall spending hours in the
backyard playing under the large apple tree.
I remember when I found the baby bluebird.
You told us not to
touch it because its mother
wouldn't feed it.
I couldn't understand how
a mother would abandon her child,
but I carefully lifted the bluebird
and put it in a box.
The backyard became its refuge.
Surely nothing would harm it.
But I cried when we went to feed it
and found it had died.
I wanted to kill every black
widow in sight.
You said it would be best
for the bluebird. I was puzzled.
The bluebird was laid to rest and
we placed a white cross on its grave.
Now, I wonder if people driving by will

see the *For Sale* sign.
You know, Grandma, I feel like that
bluebird but I know I can fly.

The Mexican Wife's Story

Often I sift through stories
puzzled at the incantations
used to suck out the evil eye
from a touched soul.
Once a distraught wife
took her husband to the *curandera*.
His eyes bled hair, insects,
strips of paper with obscenities
    on them.
The wife left the room
then the *curandera* bathed the
    husband
in olive oil mixed with goat's urine.
The *curandera* chanted,
the husband walked backwards in
    a circle.
The wife and neighboring women
recited the rosary,
lit candles outside.
After three rosaries,
the husband appeared,
eyes cleared and soul cleaned.

El Paso at the Tortilla Curtain

Restless children running back and forth
below the Santa Fe Bridge holding up your
baskets for change, how much do the passersby
drop? Do they bless you with wooden coins,
silver, or *gold*?* The Río Grande poses no
harm; now it's but a trickle of its force—the
Northerners dammed its rage. Daily, the cleaning
ladies pass and wave, the carpenters, clerks, and
professional cross here at the *tortilla* curtain
not made of iron but surely just as strong. The hot
arid sun beats upon your brow and the mountain cacti
fill the air with piercing scent. Later, the Americans
too will traverse in search of good Mexican cuisine
and fine liqueur. Are they more generous than your
own kind? The mid-day *siesta*, more a pause for the
snow cone than the nap, is your saving grace. By night
your baskets are circus lottery tries, amusement for
the drunks and the fortunate who want a sense of
lucid strife beyond the effervescent light.

---

* *Silver* is colloquial for Mexican currency, and *Gold* for American currency.

The Souls of Countless Tribes

i dream with the sun ray on my face and feel warm
i walk upon the desert sand in search of hope but
find only broken arrows and bones no longer ivory
now brittle like teeth gnashed to fight the pain
of flesh skinned for hide; the souls of countless
tribes echo among rock in the shadows of the sky
i dream with the sun ray on my face and i feel cold

The Calling of Dawn at Hueco Tanks *

Eye of God
descend upon
this earth,
let my lay
stir the
blades of
the yucca,
let this rock
shrine resound
the sacredness
of its name,
let our lineage
outlast the
calling of dawn.

* Hueco (Spanish for "empty") Tanks is an ancient religious site near El Paso.

Cristo Rey

barefoot woman
plodding up *Cristo Rey*
eyes cast low
whispering

> "Padre nuestro que está en el
> cielo..."

I ask myself: Why is she doing
    this?
but yet why am I?
I wonder astray at the sound of *los
matachines*
Is this all a dream?

> "Ave, ave, ave, María..."

Sweet fragrance of incense,
what is your source?
for we are far from the crowd

Heartwretched Man

Heartwretched man standing
by the poplar,
What's your name?
No answer?
You stand wet to your
knees with mouth agape.
—Over there.
You point to the forge
in the pass, with
eyes glazed
like ice crystals
on a fiesta snowcone.
How should I reconcile
your jubilation,
your newly found escape
through the *tortilla* curtain?
You didn't tear it down.
No, you waded through the
Río Grande, now a trickle of
its past rage.
—I come to stay.
Yes, I've heard that before.
Should I handcuff you
or perhaps I should embrace
you as El Pasoans

did thousands
who fled flying
canon balls
on that windy day?*
—*Mañana.*
Yes, *mañana* is another day.
We're here alone, wet by
our own merits and
soon to dry by our virtues.
I look the other way
and see nothing,
but my conscience,
staring out at the open,
wild horizon
painted red
by the rant
of the evening sun.

* reference to the Mexican Revolution of 1910

Tex-Mex Poetic Roundup

¡Ay Chihuahua!
Through all kinds of worry.
Through mental blight and scurry.
I'm ready, with pen by my side.
    Out, damn word, out.
    Have you no shame, no remorse?
Here perched on the edge of the chair,
waiting with bated breath, hoping,
praying for the flow to begin—
    ¡Caramba!
flash, crash, slash, click, clack—yes,
I hear the gears cranking:
word, phrase, clause,
novel, story, poem, play?
    ¡Arriba!
Rolling, rolling, rolling
though those pens are swollen
Keep those words rolling!
Rawhide!
    Yaha! Hang on! Here we go!
    Let it out, let it out, let it out!
    Rawhide!

Arcana Rejected

1.

Snow drapes the crocus by surprise
yet like the troglodyte before the
fire no veneer of ice or fright can
suppress this desire to embrace.

2.

Like the moon that pulls the tide
lust for life conquers fear and
so foliage appears.

3.

Sultry earth breeds courage to
confront taurus in the ring and
so my matador's cape tames
the passion of this flame.

Midday Escape

Six beers in *la cantina*,
a few poker games,
a taste of a woman's delight
and jail becomes home.

Kinsmen

In late spring before
the blessing of the palms,
we met. Young, full of energy,
our roots soon found earth, though
we were from different strains. East
met the Southwest and in the need for
camaraderie our friendship grew.

Naive, we as couples in the
excitement of Mexico City strolled
along *el Paseo de la Reforma* and took
in the air of ancient souls who walked upon
history in defiance of time and life. We four,
three transformed snakes from the old
and one white Russian from the North,
ate Mexico and became spirit
on the day of the dead.

Another Clay Piñata

for Glenn Spiegelhalder

You journeyed west,
a desire to follow the sun.
No serpent or dragon slain
instead mountains stopped your path.
Yucca, prickly pear
and chili peppers awoke the senses.
Air cleared of wants from the
      underground
of high shit-kicking *fiestas*.
Another clay *piñata* broken—
naked in the sun,
the toll was too hard to bear.

Part 3

—

Metaphysics

Unwrapping like an Egyptian Mummy

I recall a childhood
filled with foreign silks and chiffon.
Everyone displayed his tapestry openly
but I hid mine beneath my shirt.
Running with fright, I caught it on
my neighbor's fence and Jeff
pulled until I unwrapped like an
Egyptian mummy waiting to be
    awakened
by the gods.

Stonehenge in a Not-So-Distant Time

I register a season
outraced by passion's flight
yawed against earth
august hues,
like the lizard with
hide shed anew
quelled by fiery hail
left scalded to fathom gore.

Lovesong of a Spoken Love

You are my love and I taste your love
within my soul. Though I may fall into
the pit of lust, I trust you will help
me out and mend my weakened state.
Hold my love dear and do not forsake me.

Help me amend my worldly path that with your
love I can walk upon the truth. I kiss your
fervent lips and proclaim you are the source
of the delight in my life, now forever changed.

Stay close and guard my tongue, for though I
know you, I walk as a stranger upon the salty
land. Others have known you but I will speak the
word that will transcend you to be my love.

Stay near and help me leave my torturous memories
of death and fear. Sustain me with your clement
touch and sublime wisdom until all dread is gone,
dissipated at the coming of the morning sun.

Teach me how to love and hold my heart gently
as I walk the treacherous path of rock and sand;
together we can tread the sands of endless strife,
joined in tranquil consent.

Show me your kindness that it may blend with
my essence, that as we walk among the jaded
crowd, it will appear that we have become
tools of our own content existence.

Let us remain calm in our affliction and let no
distress torment our commission, that our house
may be enveloped with the quietness of the sea,
that our romance will outlast the flow.

Let us join our lives and preserve our course
through the night at high tide, that we may stand
stronger than before my cancerous affliction,
that no harm will brush up against our haven.

Deal gingerly with me, for once I was afflicted
and went astray; I felt my very core rent in two.
In distress, your name was upon my mouth but
then all apprehension was released.

Comfort me that my frame will be fashioned anew,
and though I flinch at what comes my way, make me
stronger with the coming of every rising tide,
that our commitment may be constant as the moon.

I long to be with you and when I close my
eyes I find solace; though smoke clouds the
pit dug for my fall along this path of hard
allegiance, I cling to what I hold precious.

Though this moment of passion may end tonight,
your love will outlast the cycles of the tide,
and the thought of you rekindles my love for
you, though you be near or far as the sky.

Alone, I embrace the memory of your love; let
wisdom bathe me like the philosophy of ancient
tribes and with my tongue I pronounce your
deeds of eternal love in a fervent sigh.

Draw near and alight my perilous path with
your wisdom of the earth and let me walk upon
the ground of ritual birth, that my forehead
will radiate my inner strength and mirth.

Although I stand out in open view, my resolve holds
me firm as I walk toward my new fate, for all
fear has dissolved as I approach the gate of life
and I feel compassion like the sun upon my face.

I stand sustained by love and close the gate
on death and hold our promise dear, the one
we agreed to openly on our day of truth
before the assembly of my peers.

Your love keeps me afloat and though I am at
sea the waters do not rise up over me; instead,
I remain content and safe in your warm embrace;
your loyalty is the rain that feeds the sea.

Pure is our love and faithful we remain in our
restrain; though trouble touches our hearth,
our commitment is stronger than the Maine
and no force shall break our strong fort.

I called out from the depths of my troubled
heart: come light, prevent the closing of
the night; and in steadfast fashion, you
drew near and diverted all my fears.

You listened and relieved my distress;
your comfort preserves me, and my love
for you fuels the font of my inner
strength; no other power can dominate.

Thoughts of loss and countless woes fill
me with regret, yet at the thought of you,
I am enveloped with the kindness that
only you can release and supply at will.

I invoke your essence and you appear,
and so we press our lips together;
the mysticism of our souls is beyond
comprehension and the love contained
grows in our enchanted state.

The Response to a Spoken Love

Listen to your inner voice and let
my thoughts roll over your mind,
let the tenets of the past fall upon
your soul and cast lust aside.

I am like the sun upon the wheat,
and like the moon at high tide I
shall not fail you, like a
constant in the galaxies.

The gate open to all tribes is my
frame and no walls shall contain the
intensity of my flame, like the
ancients who still survive.

Rain has washed over you and you
stand transformed; your cry echoes
up toward the sky and your soul
is filled with passion.

I will be with you like dried
dandelions that disperse, like
the wind that lifts rose petals
up to meet birds in flight.

I will encircle you like the isles
in the peaceful sea, like blood
that makes your heart beat, and
with time your trust will increase.

Your love will transcend your fate
and tears that flowed before shall
cease, yet your joy will break
any sense of captivity.

With the morrow, you shall sense a
new life and like blades that rustle
in a whirlwind you will feel free,
like a ship lifted from the sea.

Enjoy the fruit of the orchards
and eat berries from the vines,
for you will be content in
the serenity of the land.

Set aside your affliction; look
toward the pain and swallow your
pride, that like seed love
shall grow in its place.

I heard you call out in despair
and like the morning dew I
descended upon you to ease
the longing for compassion.

Now, a mirror reflects your
inner core; your essence should
be plain to see with self-deceit
washed from your face.

Recall that as you walk along
the path, it is now laid
for more to tread, and so
I embrace you out of love.

Far from All

far from all
        enslaved in my mind
without a soul
        I see the men
of fire and iron pass
...the war—I know like
            my mistress

I never thought
        why should I say it?
the sun has lost its fire
and I feel my thighs
        tremble with cold

Syncopated Beats

1.

I listen as your fingers
dance upon the
strings—
the *Concierto de Aranjuez*
flows with ease
like azure clouds upon
the Guadalquevir.

2.

We down cold Coronas
to the sound of
mariachis
in the Zona Rosa and
cough up the taste of
soot.

3.

Selena's last tune draws
a tear from our
clutched *machismo*,
but noticing each other
we turn to Charlie
Pride.

Paris, Let Me Linger

Distant land,
now I know you.
Your birds sing in want
and I, too, am ready.
Long have I waited
to touch you.
Your lawns are virgin satin,
yet I can only admire you by day,
for the night is more intimate.
Suffice to watch—
hummingbirds enjoy your scent,
wanting to suck the nectar
from your blossoms.
You respond—
we are content,
with the taste of blood.

Twilight

i will treasure the twilight
   of our affair
for i searched
   for a person
like the dove
   i so often saw in flight

  i would near
       but it would flee
     while i suppressed
      my lust

tenderly i hold
   the moment
     i caught
       your stare

dazzled by
   mutual bewilderment
    we touched

and in the novelty
        of the experience
            waves of passion
                raged

slowly passed
        the precious moments
            now that
                the dawn nears
            we cannot
                say goodbye

Yesterday I Saw a Naked Body

Yesterday I saw a naked body
bathing in the stream,
no one but the daffodils
and I were there.
Its softness further
than the eye could reach.
I stirred. A beauty not
surpassed by even the gods.
I saw yet could not touch.

Ménage à Trois

I am the wishbone in the
ménage à trois;
rooted in soil I hold
the two to the earth,
I am the valve
which reins the brine.

The Goodbye

You almost lit the cigarette twice
but I forced my mouth shut.
Watching your every move,
I cleared my throat.
The smoke-filled room
provoked a last word in the silence

    "Your chairs need oil.
       The backscrews need tightening."

He nodded in Japanese fashion.
Trying to cushion the air,
I found no crisp, dead leaf
to rake moisture left from a choking
    sea.

Ash Wednesday

The peach tree has begun to blossom
and the pupa awaits safely within
its cocoon,
yet upon this day
even the pigeons who without dismay
speak to each other
are aware of what
this day commemorates.
Man—
simply rides his
careless woes
revivifying laments of
yesteryear;
he so frail
and without wings
need not fret—
he has shed his cocoon.

One Afternoon in the Cathedral

Behind the shawl,
stared a face.
I moved slowly
not to make a sound.
The lady sat quietly
fingering the rosary.
Her face lit up
as the sun cut through
the stain glass windows.
Quickly she looked down at the floor
and disappeared before my eyes.

The Olive Branch

the olive branch
is free to sway
back and forth,
for with the wind
it is one;
and upon it sits
the crow of deceit
eating the fruit
but not the seed

City of Angles and Cubes

In a city of angles and cubes
Falls the shadow of the artist.
In the absurdity of his reality
Chained in the hammer—head of life
With gratification of his works he finds
    comfort.
Standing tall in his city
Above the created domain sets
The triangle, veiled in magic
Cloth, only once to be revealed.
Far beyond all intensity
Lies the ancient pyramid,
Filled with precious stones
He has gathered through the years,
In the foreground amongst the angles
Painted red with blue stars
Rests the cubic square,
Transforming into an octagon
As a drum ready to be played.
Peacefully guarded by the triangle
Stands the rectangle patiently
Awaiting the music of
The drum to be subdued.

So Where's Kansas?

for Micheal King

I bite into ice
yellow cantaloupe
and walk upon
lightning rods
as I look for
the ruby slippers;
stuck in mud,
divorced from Toto,
I wait for
Dorothy to
take me to the
land of Oz.

Memories

for Marilyn A. Coulters

joy of life,
warmth of friends;
a gentle breeze
released in time,
memories.

Transition

for Woody Elrod

Now, commune with me;
let us restore the rapport
lost by transition.

Nocturnal Union

moon, bathe me anew
and though I lay in
        dismay
I embrace your hue

Touching the Sea Gull

i thought i
touched the soaring
sea gull
but it was
only man-in-the-moon
marigolds reflected
upward into
the depleted
ozone layer

Venice Beach

Stranded on Venice Beach
I await the tide as
the moon reaches down
and sugars the salty sea.
The coolness of morning
    greets
me without Van Gogh's lust
    for life.
Expecting the frothy foam
to choke me, I
slide into oblivion.

Lying with Zeus

Naked, skin
taut, I lie
next to Zeus.
I lick his face
and give him drink
from my mouth.
I bathe his body
with juniper berries
and dry the wet with
eucalyptus leaves.
Flesh smooth
as rose petals,
I wait for
life to enter me.

ModernCauldron

We surround our cauldron
and feed the fire our fate.
"What can you add to spice up
the stew?" Add self-hate,
vengeance, and indifference.
The mint, bay leaf, and laurel
curry the entrails of our brew.
Together we survive the famine—
our frailty melted down and
ionized, the broth is now rich
in protein, and as we consume
collective essence of our creation,
the nature of our wisdom leaps into
poetic conscience of invention.

The Coming of AIDS

Stripped, exhausted, weak—left like
bones in Auschwitz, I count my
friends and mount their names
on the imaginary black wall beside
the vets standing in triumphant display.
Some also fought, but now that we
are not at war they are held in
contempt and are purged from
twisted colons like bad garlic
lodged deep in the bowels.
Convenience to kill, endorsed
by the cross—now the white
hoods search the cells for
their cathartic plunge. No one
sees their reflection in those
they choose to defame—how
strange—even deer know that
daffodils are lethal in their
seemingly state of grace. Public
figures shroud themselves in
ballistic rhetoric and feed the
hunger for hate—echoes of Hitler,
the Inquisitor, and the Holy
Crusade. "Let them die" —

"Let's cleanse our cities of
such utter scum." — I gasp
and hold back the tide of tears
as I traverse the patched quilts
that commemorate the lives of
hope, the struggle for self-love,
to say nothing of the talent, the
energy of youth. But here on this
ground, this cloth connects their
souls and though the grief weighs
it down, its spirit is light
and it transcends the pall of
constant decay. Now, thousands
embrace the meaning of love, that
like a mystical *aurora borealis*
that electrifies those who are in
awe of its strength unite to move
the spiritual transformation
upon this salted earth.

Guardians of Wake

We are on the edge and
inhale the vileness of
the state, and though we
dress the living and color
with our visions, we are
placed as midwives at the
gate to care for the broken,
filed like sod blocks to
reconstruct Solomon's
     temple,
yet quartering and burning
us at the stake cannot
contain the cataclysmic
energy that pulls us
together like a tribe
searching for its soul.

Shrouded

for Nellie Valdez

I lay frozen in time
and awake shrouded
in cob webs, fastened
to the bed; no muscle
can release me from
this snare and though
I breathe and perceive
through this silky
vellum which encases
me there is little I
can do to escape, yet
no dread touches me,
for this strain has
no power over me.

What Value Does Wisdom Have?

What value comes of this lineage
if not wisdom and a sense of right
that rings sound in your sight?
Truth is hidden in the parable
yet only the wise hear the words
of its riddle. How does it come
about? Is it fear or love of
truth that sets you upon your
path? Heed the lessons that are
handed from age to age that in the
moral you may sense what is honest
and what is false. Though a net
is cast at your feet, your footing
is safe from the pit, that those
who reach for the sky are short
and fall into the sea. A solemn
voice cries out in the street,
the doors are closed, the shutters
too, that the echo reverberates
and turns and twists like the
lost in the labyrinth of old.
What counsel will do them good

that no whirlwind can shake
their stand? What drives their
search for a dwelling replete
with fruit if not the soul's
desire to be whole?

Así

Eye of the sun
warm my soul
as i sing my
corrido and
dance with
the breeze
to follow
my bliss